The Gringo's Culture Guide to Chile

What you should know

before arriving in Chile

Written by Joe "Pepe" Rawlinson

pepeschile.com

Copyright © 2011 Joe Rawlinson

First Edition

ISBN 978-1456350239

All rights reserved. This book contains material protected under International and Federal Copyright Laws and Treaties. Any unauthorized reprint or use of this material is prohibited. No part of this book may be reproduced or transmitted in any form or by any means, electronic or mechanical, including photocopying, recording, or by any information storage and retrieval system without express written permission from the author.

Table of Contents

Introduction...4

Chapter 1: Chile..5

Chapter 2: Chilean People..............................28

Chapter 3: Life in Chile..................................36

Chapter 4: Food..61

Chapter 5: Money..71

Chapter 6: Travel..76

Chapter 7: Communicating.............................84

Conclusion..89

Additional Reading...90

Glossary...92

Introduction

Chile is one of the Earth's most beautiful countries. In this single, skinny stretch of land along South America's Pacific coast, you can experience everything from the world's driest desert to snow capped volcanoes, Antarctic penguins, and a warm and loving people.

Modern Chile is a product of a storied past that has produced a proud and independent people with a culture that is uniquely Chilean.

Chile stands as a shining star of opportunity and success among South American countries and its influence and products have probably already touched your life regardless of where you live in the world.

One of the joys of visiting Chile is immersion in the culture, nuances, and beauties of this marvelous country. Unfortunately, unless you are prepared, these same opportunities can become stumbling blocks.

This culture guide will give you the insights you need to hit the ground running in Chile and better understand the new world you will be experiencing.

Chapter 1: Chile

Legend of Chile's Origin

One of Chile's legends is how the country was created by the hand of God:

In the beginning of time, God created the wonders of the world. When he was finished, he saw that he had many leftover pieces. He had parts of rivers and valleys, of oceans and lakes, of glaciers and deserts, of mountains and forests, and of meadows and hills. Rather than let such beauty go to waste, God put them all together and cast them to the most remote corner of the Earth. This is how Chile was born.

Torres del Paine

The diversity of Chile's geography and climates attest to the validity of this legend. Where else can you find both the driest desert on Earth and huge ice glaciers? Chile is a land of contrasts and beauties found nowhere else on Earth.

In reference to the legend's "remote corner of the earth" statement, many Chileans today refer to Chile as the "end of the world."

In fact, a large part of Chile is found farther south than Australia or even South Africa, both of which share the southern reaches of the globe's Southern Hemisphere.

Why the Name Chile?

Name Origins

According to Wikipedia[1], there are numerous ideas of how Chile's name originated:

> *According to one theory, the Incas of Peru, who had failed to conquer the Araucanians, called the valley of the Aconcagua "Chili" by corruption of the name of a tribal chief ("cacique") called Tili, who ruled the area at the time of the Incan conquest.*
>
> *Another theory points to the similarity of the valley of the Aconcagua with that of the Casma Valley in Peru, where there was a town and valley named Chili.*
>
> *Other theories say Chile may derive its name from the indigenous Mapuche word chilli, which may mean "where the land ends," "the deepest point of the Earth," or "sea gulls;" or*

---

1   http://en.wikipedia.org/wiki/Chile#Etymology

from the Quechua chin, "cold", or the Aymara tchili, meaning "snow."

Another meaning attributed to chilli is the onomatopoeic cheele-cheele—the Mapuche imitation of a bird call. The Spanish conquistadors heard about this name from the Incas and the few survivors of Diego de Almagro's first Spanish expedition south from Peru in 1535-36 called themselves the "men of Chilli."

Name Facts

While there are various possible origins of Chile's name, there are a few things that are certain:

- Chile isn't spelled Chili today unless you are speaking French.
- Chile isn't called that because the country's shape is long and could look like a chili pepper.
- Chile's official name is *La República de Chile*, or Republic of Chile.

Key Chile Facts

Chileans are extremely proud of their country, so you'll automatically be in their favor if you know a little about their country.

Capital: Santiago

Official Country Name: República de Chile

Population: 16,746,491 (July 2010 est.)

Life Expectancy: *total population:* 77.53 years
male: 74.26 years
female: 80.96 years

Ethnic groups: white and white-Amerindian 95.4%, Mapuche 4%, other indigenous groups 0.6%

Religions: Roman Catholic 70%, Evangelical 15.1%, Jehovah's Witness 1.1%, other Christian 1%, other 4.6%, none 8.3% (2002 census)

Time Zone: *time difference:* UTC-4 (1 hour ahead of Washington, DC during Standard Time)
daylight saving time: +1hr, begins second Sunday in October; ends second Sunday in March

Chief Agriculture Products: grapes, apples, pears, onions, wheat, corn, oats, peaches, garlic, asparagus, beans; beef, poultry, wool; fish; timber

Primary Industries: copper, other minerals, foodstuffs, fish processing, iron and steel, wood and wood products, transport equipment, cement, textiles

The national flower of Chile is the Copihue, also known as the Chilean Bellflower or Chilean Glory Flower. The flower has six petals and grows in the forests of southern Chile.

Copihue

Copper

Chile has over a third of all the copper reserves in the world. This abundance of copper has turned it into Chile's major export.

Copper has been mined in northern Chile since before pre-colonial times and before Chile was even a country. The mineral-rich northern territory of Chile was won from Peru and Bolivia in the War of the Pacific in the late 1800's.

The northern Atacama desert is home to some of the world's largest copper mines like Chuquicamata. Although northern Chile has the majority of Chile's copper mines, the large *El Teniente* mine is found in central Chile, south of Santiago.

Chuquicamata

During Chilean president Salvador Allende's rule in the early 1970s, Chile nationalized the nation's copper mines and formed the National Copper Corporation of Chile (CODELCO).

The state-owned firm CODELCO is the world's largest copper-producing company. Chile has enough copper to mine for 200 more years.

Since Chile's copper mining is nationalized, the profits and dividends from copper production go to benefit the state.

Due to copper's dominance as Chile's primary export, the country's economy follows a boom-and-bust cycle that varies with the price of copper on the world market.

Geography

Chile is a long, skinny country that runs along the west coast of South America. Chile borders Argentina on the East, Peru and Bolivia on the North, and has 6,435 kilometers (4,000 miles) of coast on the Pacific Ocean. Several Pacific islands like Easter Island and the San Fernando Islands are part of the country as well.

Chile has a long-standing claim of 1,236,000 km² (768,000 sq miles) of Antarctica.

The magnificent Andes mountains are a product of the tectonic activity along this part of the Ring of Fire that circles the Pacific Ocean. This gives Chile both impressive mountain peaks and active volcanoes along its length. Earthquakes are common in Chile but most are minor. Chileans refer to these minor earthquakes as *temblores*, not full-blown *terremotos*.

Although most earthquakes are minor, Chile does have the ominous claim of having the strongest earthquake ever recorded. On May 22, 1960, a 9.5 magnitude quake centered near Valdivia, Chile had repercussions reaching all the way to Japan, Hawaii, and the Philippines, killing nearly 2,000 people worldwide.

More recently, an 8.8 magnitude earthquake struck north of Concepción, Chile on February 27, 2010. The quake and subsequent tsunami killed over 500 people and left an estimated 500,000 people homeless.

Regions

Chile consists of 15 regions which are political divisions like other countries' provinces or states. These regions are most commonly referred to by their numbers, except for the *Region Metropolitana* (RM) which contains the capital city, Santiago.

XV   Arica and Parinacota
I   Tarapacá
II   Antofagasta
III   Atacama
IV   Coquimbo
V   Valparaíso
RM   Region Metropolitana (Santiago)
VI   O'Higgins
VII   Maule
VIII   Biobío
IX   Araucanía
XIV   Los Ríos
X   Los Lagos
XI   Aisén
XII   Magallanes and Antártica Chilena

The regions used to be in numerical order from North to South. However, in 2007, Chile added two new regions, *Los Ríos* (XIV) and *Arica* (XV). You'll notice that XIII is skipped since the *Region Metropolitana* was the thirteenth region.

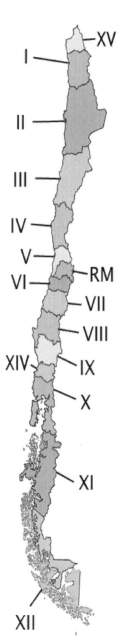

Weather and Climate

Chile is a country of vast climate extremes. Due to Chile's long slender shape spanning from Peru in the north to Antarctica in the south, you'll experience a very different climate depending on what part of the country you visit. As a general rule, the farther north, the hotter and drier the climate. As you head south, you'll see a cooler and wetter climate. Rainfall is more frequent during Chile's winter months.

Seasons

Chile sits in the southern hemisphere, and as such, its seasons are generally these:

- Summer: December - February
- Fall: March - May
- Winter: June - August
- Spring: September - November

Northern Climate

The Atacama Desert

Chile's northernmost regions are characterized by a dry, arid climate. The world's driest desert, the Atacama, defines the northernmost part of the country. Rainfall is so sparse here that some places haven't seen any precipitation in years. As is typical of desert climates, there is little seasonal change during the year and daily high temperatures decline significantly overnight, particularly at higher elevations.

Southern Climate

The southern extreme of Chile is prone to frequent rainfall, with winter months being the wettest. This humid and damp climate leads to a lush green landscape.

Volcán Osorno

Central Valley

The central valley enjoys a Mediterranean climate. Summers are warm and dry with little precipitation. Winters are cooler and deliver frequent rain showers. This very moderate climate encourages the fertile agriculture of this region. Summers rarely get hotter than 100° F or 37° C. Winter temperatures in this region approach freezing on occasion (0° C or 32° F), but most of the snow stays in the mountains.

Andes Mountains

The eastern border of Chile is the Andean mountain range. The climate here is a combination of climates typical of higher elevations, and depending on the latitude you'll be visiting, you may see climates that are similar to those of the North, South, or Central Valley.

Andes Mountains

Islands

In addition to the islands found in the south, Chile has numerous islands far off shore in the Pacific Ocean. These include notable islands like Easter Island and the Juan Fernández Islands. Due to these islands being widely dispersed, the climate varies accordingly.

Coast

Coastal regions typically mirror the region of the country in which they are located. That general climate is modified by oceanic effects.

Chilean Coast near Viña del Mar

Antarctica

Chile has territorial claims on parts of Antarctica. This region is characterized by ice and extreme cold temperatures year-round.

Chilean Flag

The design of the Chile flag was influenced by the flag of the United States. The Chile flag has two horizontal bands with white on top and red on the bottom. A blue square sits in the upper left corner of the flag and contains a white 5 pointed star.

Chilean Flag

The red on the Chile flag represents the blood spilled in its fight for independence. The white represents the snow-covered Andes that guard the eastern border of Chile. The blue is for the color of the sky. The star represents the governmental powers as they watch over the country.

Chile versus Texas Flag

At first glance, the Chilean and Texas flags look almost identical. They can be easily confused since they each contain the same elements: a lone star on a blue background with horizontal red and white bands.

Texas Flag

Chile's flag was born of a rich history and went through several versions before arriving at its current form in October 1817.

The Texan flag was officially adopted on January 24, 1839, as the final national flag of the Republic of Texas. Chile's flag predates the Texas flag by 21 years.

On a Pole

The flag pole must be white and the flag must hang from the top of the pole. If the Chile flag is displayed with those of other countries, they should all be of equal size and raised to the same height. Also in this case, the flag should be raised first and lowered last.

Freely Hanging

The Chile flag can be displayed hanging either vertically or horizontally from a building or wall. In both cases, the blue square should be to the viewer's upper left.

Legal Obligation to Fly Chilean Flag

According to Chilean law, citizens are required to display the flag on certain national holidays including independence day (September 18). If Chileans display the flag incorrectly, they can be fined by the police.

Famous Chileans

You'll see famous Chilean names in many places throughout the country. Historical figures and those from the arts and politics will appear on street and city names. You'll see references to sports and entertainment figures on television, the newspapers, and other media.

Historical

Pedro de Valdivia – Spanish conquistador that founded Santiago
Arturo Prat – Chilean naval hero who died in battle during War of the Pacific
Bernardo O'Higgins – one of Chile's founding fathers
Diego Portales – early Chilean statesman

Entertainment

Don Francisco – television host of *Sábado Gigante* in Miami
Lucho Gatica – Chilean bolero singer
Myriam Hernández – singer
Claudio Arrau – Chilean pianist
Cristián de la Fuente – actor in television and film

Literature

Pablo Neruda – Nobel Prize winning poet (1971)
Gabriela Mistral – Nobel Prize winning poet (1945)
Vicente Huidobro – poet
Isabel Allende – author and niece of deposed president Salvador Allende

Sports

Fernando Gonzalez – tennis player and Olympic medalist

Nicolás Massú – tennis player and two time Olympic gold medalist
Marcelo Rios – famed tennis player that reached No 1. in the world in 1998
Luis Ivan Zamorano – one of Chile's greatest soccer players, now retired
Marcelo Salas – popular soccer player nicknamed El Matador, now retired
Manuel Pellegrini – former soccer player, now coach of Malaga CF

Politics

Salvador Allende – socialist president that was overthrown by Pinochet
Augusto Pinochet – general who lead coup over Allende and became dictator
Michelle Bachelet – first woman president of Chile elected in 2006

Augusto Pinochet

If you want to broach a sensitive subject, talk to a Chilean about Augusto Pinochet. This man and his actions defined a generation and directly impacted the Chile we know today.

Augusto Pinochet was Chile's head of state from 1973 to 1990. How he came into power and the way he ruled the country are sources of much controversy.

In 1970, Senator Salvador Allende, a Marxist and member of Chile's Socialist Party, won a three-way contest and was named President by the Chilean Congress. He proceeded to nationalize private industries, copper mines, and banks.

Under Allende, domestic production declined; severe shortages of consumer goods, food, and manufactured products were widespread; and inflation reached 1,000% per year.

A military coup overthrew Allende on September 11, 1973. As the armed forces bombarded the presidential palace, Allende reportedly committed suicide. A military government, led by General Augusto Pinochet, took over control of the country.

The regime was marked by serious human rights violations. Chile's government says at least 3,197 people were killed for political reasons during Pinochet's rule. Thousands more Chileans were exiled to remote corners of the country or fled to other countries for refuge.

A new Constitution was approved on September 11, 1980, and General Pinochet became President of the Republic for an 8-year term. During this time, Chile moved toward a largely free market economy that fostered an increase in domestic and foreign private investment.

In a 1988 referendum, the Chilean people voted to end the military regime and General Pinochet was denied a second 8-year term as president. In 1989, Christian Democrat Patricio Aylwin, the candidate of a coalition of 17 political parties called the *Concertación*, was elected president, taking office in 1990.

Pinochet remained Commander in Chief of the Chilean army until 1998, thereafter becoming a senator for life. During the last years of his life, lawsuits began that would bring Pinochet to trial for his human right violations, tax evasion, and embezzlement. Nevertheless, he was never convicted and died in 2006.

Pinochet's death brought to the surface the great emotions and dark history of his rule. Some Chileans praise him for saving Chile from communist rule since he displaced the socialist Allende. Others deplore him for his oppressive and often violent regime.

Famous Chilean Songs

Chile has its official national anthem, the *Himno Nacional*, and then the unofficial song which all those that love Chile sing: *Si Vas Para Chile* by Chito Faró. You will impress any Chilean if you can sing these songs, or even quote parts of them.

Himno Nacional (National Anthem)

Puro, Chile, es tu cielo azulado,
Puras brisas te cruzan también,
Y tu campo de flores bordado
Es la copia feliz del Edén.
Majestuosa es la blanca montaña
Que te dio por baluarte el Señor,
Y ese mar que tranquilo te baña
Te promete futuro esplendor.

Dulce Patria, recibe los votos
Con que Chile en tus aras juró
Que o la tumba serás de los libres
O el asilo contra la opresión.

Si Vas Para Chile

Si vas para Chile, te ruego que pases
por donde vive mi amada
es una casita muy linda y chiquita
que esta en las faldas de un cerro enclavada,
la adornan las parras y cruza un estero
al frente hay un sauce que llora
que llora porque yo la quiero.

*Si vas para Chile, te ruego viajero
le digas a ella que de amor me muero.
El pueblito se llama Las Condes
y esta junto a los cerros y el cielo.
Y si miras de lo alto hacia el valle
tu veras que lo cruza un estero.
Campesinos y gentes del pueblo
te saldran al encuentro, viajero
y verás como quieren en Chile
al amigo, cuando es forastero.
Si vas para Chile, te ruego viajero,
le digas a ella que de amor me muero.*

You can listen to the music of both the national anthem and *Si Vas Para Chile* online at pepeschile.com.

Common Misconceptions and Truths

There are many misconceptions of what Chile is and what it is not.

Historically, Chileans don't tango; Argentinians do. Chile's national dance is called *la cueca,* although you will see a growing number of tango dance halls in Chile.

Chileans don't wear sombreros like you'd see in Mexico. Traditional Chilean cowboys, called *huasos*, do have a sombrero-like hat but the typical Chilean on the street is more likely to wear a baseball cap.

You won't find typical Mexican food like burritos or enchiladas being made in Chilean homes. (See Chapter 4 for typical Chilean foods.)

Dancing *la cueca* in traditional *huaso* attire

Chileans don't speak Portuguese. That would be Brazil or Portugal. (See Chapter 7 for more on Chilean Spanish.)

Chile has a varied climate but definitely does not have any tropical jungles with monkeys swinging in the trees like you'd find in the Amazon.

Chileans are not all dark-skinned nor do they all live in houses made of adobe or mud. Most Chileans have a European ancestry, are relatively fair-skinned with dark hair and brown eyes.

The following chapters will cast aside any remaining misconceptions and give you a picture of what Chile really is.

Chapter 2: Chilean People

Straight Talkers

Chileans don't pull any punches when talking to you. They are blunt and frank in their statements. For example, don't be surprised if you visit someone you haven't seen in a while and they calmly state "My, you're looking fat" or if you're lucky, "You're getting skinny." While this may seem like taboo in other cultures, Chileans just call it like they see it. Their statements aren't intended as an insult, but rather a statement of fact.

Last Names

Like most Latin American countries, Chileans have two last names. This usually means that each person has four names in total, a first, middle, and two surnames. The first surname is the person's father's last name. The second surname is the mother's maiden name. A Chilean will usually go by one of their first names and then the father's surname.

For example, Chile's first female president, Michelle Bachelet's full name is Verónica Michelle Bachelet Jeria. Bachelet is her father's family name, and Jeria is that of her mother.

When Chilean women marry, they don't take the last name of the husband. However, sometimes they may tack on the husband's last name on the very end preceded by a *de*. For example, if Michelle were to marry a man by the last name of Tapia, she may be called Verónica Michelle Bachelet Jeria de Tapia.

When referring to a family, you'd use the last name of the father followed by the mother. So the previous example would be the Tapia Bachelet family.

Nicknames

Chileans love their nicknames. While a person's given name may be one thing, odds are they have a nickname that everyone else calls them. So you'll hear a Patricio called *Pato* or even a chubby boy called *Gordito*. Nicknames are either derivatives of the given name or reflect a physical characteristic of the person.

Social Classes

Chile's society is divided into social classes. These don't have an official, declared hierarchy but it permeates the country and affects how Chileans interact with others. Chileans are divided by their income. These social levels help determine everything from where someone lives to how they spend their weekends. The working class Chileans will most often only associate with others in their socio-economic level.

Many of the rich Chileans live very comfortable lives separate from the general population. They have large houses in exclusive parts of Santiago or the other parts of the country. Their children attend private schools. Many of those with money in Chile come from families that have long owned vineyards, businesses, or other interests. A new breed of wealthy Chilean is emerging but they tend to follow the same lifestyle as their "old money" counterparts.

Chile has a large middle class. These Chileans own or rent their homes and often have a car. They vacation in Chile and live comfortable lives. A middle class Chilean may make $1200 USD per month. An upper middle class family may earn $1800 USD a month.

The poor in Chile are often those that work in agriculture or other manually intensive jobs. They may live in overcrowded apartment buildings or even simple homes without electricity in the countryside. These families may barely subsist on minimum wage.

Minimum Wage in Chile

The minimum wage a worker in Chile can earn each month is set by law and usually adjusted yearly based on inflation. As of 2009, the minimum wage in Chile is $165,000 Chilean pesos or about $300 USD per month.

This is the minimum amount a worker will earn for full time work where full time work doesn't exceed 45 hours a week.

Chile has one of the higher minimum wages in Latin America. However, recent critics have noted that the raise in the wage hasn't kept pace with inflation and thus the buying power has actually decreased.

There is discussion in Chile about an "ethical minimum wage" that acknowledges how much money someone really needs to live on. Currently this unofficial ethical minimum wage is $250,000 pesos or about $450 USD. The debate raging in Chile about the ethical minimum wage is whether the official wage should just be raised or if the state should subsidize the difference with the working poor.

Understated

Chileans by nature are mostly low-key and understated individuals. They are not extravagant or over-the-top. Even those with money don't tend to flaunt it. Sure, they may have a big house, but it is also behind a big wall so no one can see it.

Warming Up

At first, Chileans may seem standoff-ish and not very interested in opening up to you. However, once you get to know a Chilean, they will be your best friend and be generous in giving and caring for you. Show a genuine interest in the Chileans you meet and try to ask about the things they care about. If you drop any assumptions or prejudices you have about Chile, the Chileans will be much more likely to be friendly back to you.

Machismo

Traditionally, Chile has been a male dominated society. This is slowly changing but there is still a dominant *machismo* attitude towards women. Typically, women stay home and care for the house and kids. The women that work in professional arenas are most likely paid less than their male counterparts.

As Chile evolves into a more modern society, some of these stereotypes are starting to break down but you will still see behavior or attitudes that hold on to the mindsets of yesterday. These behaviors manifest themselves in how women are treated in the workplace, on the street, and especially in the home.

Foreigners

Chileans are fascinated by foreigners, particularly those with blond hair and blue eyes. As a foreigner, you will be an oddity and an object of curiosity to those around you. A common reaction on the street may be people yelling English phrases at you that they either learned in school or from movies.

Chileans dress in conservative colors like blacks, browns, and grays. If you wear bright colors or loud outfits, you will stand out in the crowd and this may draw unwanted attention.

Chile's Neighbors

Chile has a storied history with its neighboring countries. The War of the Pacific in the late 1800's ended with Chile defeating both Peru and Bolivia. With this victory, Chile earned a large concession of land that is now the northern part of the country. This resulted in Bolivia losing its access to the sea and Peru conceding a chunk of its territory. The animosity between these countries remains to this day with continued border and maritime boundary disputes.

Chile shares a very long border with Argentina and has had tense relationships over border disputes in southern Patagonia. Although those disputes almost resulted in armed conflict in the 1970's, they were resolved peacefully and today relationships are significantly better between the two countries.

Many Chileans have a negative attitude towards those from Argentina, Peru, and Bolivia.

Santiago vs. the Rest of Chile

Over a third of all Chileans live in or around Santiago. Because of its massive size, Santiago's culture is often different from the rest of the country. Large city life makes *Santiaguinos* hurried and stressed. Santiago is characterized by a high population density and lots of traffic. Those outside the capital city enjoy a slightly less hectic life and are often more friendly and hospitable.

Mapuches

Chile's primary indigenous people are called the Mapuches. Originally called the *Araucanos* by the Spanish conquistadors, they successfully repelled invasion and were known as fierce fighters. While the Mapuches traditionally lived in south-central Chile, they can now be found throughout the country and comprise about 4% of the population.

Military Service

Until recently, all Chilean men were subject to obligatory military service. This system was rife with poor treatment of conscripts and has been changed to focus on having a volunteer, professional military. While Chile now relies on volunteers to staff its ranks, it still reserves the right to draft any number of men it needs to fill shortfalls.

Maids

Maids are often referred to as *nanas* and typically cook, clean, and even care for the kids. Not everyone has a maid. Generally those in upper class homes have paid servants like a maid that live with the family. Other times, *nanas* may only work during the day. If you are living as a foreigner in Chile, you may very well be able to afford to hire a maid to help around your home. You'll be able to hire an immigrant maid, like someone from Peru, for significantly less than a Chilean.

Marriage

Chilean law requires that a couple be married by an official from the Civil Registry. This is a very simple civil ceremony. The man will dress in a suit and the woman in a dress (not a wedding gown). They are accompanied by witnesses. Once the bride and groom sign the registry, they are legally married.

While some couples will only have a civil marriage, the vast majority will have a religious ceremony with its accompanying pageantry. This event may follow quickly after the civil ceremony or come weeks later. Most Chileans are Catholic and are married in the church surrounded by friends and family. After the religious ceremony, a reception may be held at a private home where there will be dancing, cake, and traditional celebrations.

Due to Chile's conservative Catholic history, divorce was only recently legalized in 2004. Before that, individuals that had separated would start a new life with another partner and even have children together while still technically being married to their previous partner.

Typical Work Day

The typical work day is generally from 8:30 a.m. to 6:00 p.m. depending on the business. Nevertheless, employees may often stay late to complete assigned tasks. Particularly in Santiago, this long work day is combined with a lengthy and arduous commute. This can add an hour or two each way to the work day.

Those outside the city, especially those in agriculture, will work longer hours, particularly during harvest season.

Chapter 3: Life in Chile

How to Greet a Chilean

Male Chileans will greet each other with a handshake if they are unfamiliar with each other. A man greeting a woman, or two women meeting will greet with a kiss on the cheek. More informal relationships lead to greetings with a big hug (*un abrazo*) for men and a kiss on the cheek for women.

Un abrazo

Pointing with the Lips

Instead of pointing with the index finger, Chileans will use their lips to point. Lips are puckered and pointed in the direction of interest. Pointing with the lips can indicate a single direction, or moving the lips can indicate a motion or larger area.

All about the Family

Chilean society revolves around the family. Many homes have multiple generations living in them. So don't be surprised to see parents with their kids, a grandparent or two, plus a random cousin living under the same roof.

Chilean Family

Because of the importance Chileans put on the family, it becomes the hub of socializing. For example, friends will get together for a cookout or *asado* at a family's home to celebrate a birthday, holiday, or just the weekend.

Families will also travel together for vacations or weekend trips to the beach or mountains.

Friends

The best way for a Chilean to get to know you is to invite you home for an *asado* or other gathering. This is a sign of respect and you should accept an invitation to visit someone's home if invited. Chileans are more apt to bring someone home than they are to take them out to eat at a restaurant.

Pituto

Chilean society is built on the back of social connections. These networks of relationships are formed amongst family, neighbors, co-workers, college buddies, and childhood friends.

Pituto is the Chilean slang for connections that come in handy in a variety of circumstances.

There is a saying in Chile, *es mejor tener amigos que plata*, which means "It is better to have friends than money."

Do you need a new job? *Pituto* will help you find it through an old friend.

Want a private tour of the presidential palace? *Pituto* helps when your friend works there.

Having a hard time getting a reservation during the busy travel season? Don't worry, *pituto* happens to have a cousin that works down there and can get you in.

Pituto is so pervasive that often times being on the outside is that much harder — for a gringo or a Chilean.

So just remember: friends are better than money in Chile.

What to Talk About

At first, it may seem hard to break the ice when talking with Chileans. Talk about topics that won't get you in trouble: family, the weather, places to visit in Chile, your home, etc. Stay away from politics and very far away from Pinochet. He was the military dictator that overthrew the socialist Allende in 1973. Chileans either love Pinochet or hate him. Don't get caught in the middle of that. Change the topic or listen patiently.

Nightlife in Chile

Chileans love to dance, and not just the national dance, *la cueca*. Nighttime activities may include heading to a local disco to dance until the early morning hours.

You're a *Gringo*

Chileans will call you a *gringo* to your face and when talking about you. This is fine. Using the word *gringo* in Chile doesn't have any negative connotations. You can even joke and say that you are from *gringolandia*. Feel free to use your gringo status to start conversations and break the ice.

You're an Uncle or Aunt

When you befriend a Chilean family that has younger kids, they will start calling you *tío* (uncle) or *tía* (aunt) even though you aren't really related to them. It is both a term of endearment and a compliment.

Punctuality

Chileans have two standards for timeliness. If they have a business appointment, they will typically be on time. For personal gatherings, parties, or social events, Chileans will be late. If you show up to one of these on time, you'll be the first one there. Don't be surprised if someone doesn't show up for a get-together without letting you know. Time in the social arena is relative and flexible so plan accordingly.

Traditional Games

There are several traditional Chilean games and toys that you may enjoy during your time in Chile.

El Trompo (Top)

The traditional Chilean top is made of wood and has a metal prong sticking out of the end. String or twine is coiled around the top. Kids will play with their tops in the streets. Some games include trying to keep the top spinning in a defined circle. Others will launch their tops and try to knock competitor's tops out of the circle.

El Volantín (Kite)

Kite flying is a favorite pastime in Chile. Chileans like to make their own kites from balsa wood and tissue paper. These are then attached to large spools of string as seen in the picture.

Kite Flying

One competition with kites is to try and cut down another's kite by wrapping the string around the other kite, cutting the line. Real competitors often coat their string in glass to increase their chances of earning a victory known as a commission.

El Emboque

The name *emboque* comes from the Spanish verb *embocar*, which means "to put into the mouth." This toy consists of a heavy, bell-shaped piece of wood with a hole in the bottom. It is attached to a wooden stick by a string coming out of the top of the bell. The stick fits into hole in the bottom of the bell. Play begins by holding the stick and letting the bell fall the length of the string. The objective is to flip the bell up from the hanging position and catch it on the end of the stick, with the stick entering the hole in the bottom of the bell. It can be quite challenging!

Rayuela

Rayuela or *tejo* is a traditional Chilean game typical of rural Chile that has been played since colonial times. The game of *Rayuela* most resembles the game of horse shoes.

It is important to note that there is another game called *rayuela* played by Chilean children which is really just hopscotch. However, the traditional Chilean *rayuela* is very different from this childhood version.

The objective is throw your *tejo*, a disk or marker like a rock, so that it lands on the target.

The target is a wooden box less than a square meter in size and about a board's width high. This box is filled with mud and a taut, white string is stretched across the surface in the middle.

A player will stand a designated distance from the box

and throw the *tejo* trying to get it to land on the string. The most points are awarded to the player who lands closest to the string or on top of it.

Soccer

Chileans' love of soccer is developed from their very early years. Like most of the world, soccer is the biggest sport in Chile. Kids of all ages play soccer in the street, empty fields, or anywhere there is a ball.

A Game of Soccer

Some areas like schools or churches have little soccer fields in the back. These *canchas* are a smaller playing area made of concrete and facilitate games of *baby fútbol*, or baby soccer.

Almost every kid on the street will ask you, ¿*de qué equipo soi?* or "What's your team?" Chile has three big soccer clubs: Colo Colo, la Universidad de Chile, and la Universidad Católica. Although these are the most popular, there are dozens of teams and many huge soccer stadiums throughout Chile.

Regardless of their individual favorite team, all Chileans unite to cheer on their national soccer team. When the

Chilean team plays internationally, the entire country holds its breath as it waits for the outcome. For major games like the World Cup, work stops when the Chilean team plays. Victories are followed by huge celebrations in the streets and at common gathering places like *Plaza Italia* in Santiago.

Outdoor Activities

Chile's varied landscapes offer countless outdoor activities such as hiking, biking, skiing, rafting, etc. A lot of these activities, if hosted by a guide, are expensive and not affordable to the typical Chilean. The summer months see a migration of Chileans out of the cities and into the countryside or beaches to enjoy the outdoors.

Types of Housing

Chileans live in a wide variety of housing. Older, traditional Chilean homes imitate the Spanish style with a courtyard in the middle of the home. In urban areas, many live in high rise apartments. In the suburbs, people live in duplexes and row houses often made of concrete. You'll also find apartment

Row houses in Valparaiso

complexes in lower income areas called *blocks* which are groups of apartment buildings a few stories tall.

As you move into the countryside, land owners with money have larger homes on *parcelas* or parcels of land with orchards and even domesticated farm animals.

Most private homes have a fence around them. Typically, this is a metal cast-iron fence with a gate that separates the house from the street. While some homes have a bell on the outside gate, you may have to yell *halo*, acting as a human bell, to get the attention of those inside.

Estufas

Most homes in Chile don't have a central heating system. This means homes can get very cold in the winter months. Most Chileans have at least one *estufa*, or literally, "a stove" to keep them warm. This isn't a traditional cooking stove. It is often a propane-powered space heater with an open flame. These stout rectangular contraptions house a large propane canister that can be replaced when used. Gas salesman will travel around neighborhoods with their trucks full of propane tanks to sell.

Don't expect an *estufa* in every room of a Chilean home. Typically, the main living area is heated and bedrooms

45

are not. So be sure you have warm pajamas and blankets for the winter season.

Califont

The *califont* is the typical Chilean water heater. This warms the water by passing it through a series of pipes that cross back and forth through the path of a propane fueled flame. Thus the hot water is on demand and not stored in a large tank like a typical North American water heater.

This creates an interesting challenge in making sure you get the right amount of hot water. The faster the water is coming through the pipe, the less time it has to warm up and the cooler it will be. Turning up the hot water in the shower may not have the anticipated result.

Depending on the home's *califont,* you may need to light the pilot light before you jump in the shower or you may have a rather cold surprise. More modern apartments and buildings will have self-lighting *califonts* or even water heaters with ready-to-use hot water in a tank.

Voltage and Plugs

Electricity in Chile is 220 Volts, alternating at 50 cycles per second. If you travel to Chile with a device that does not accept 220 Volts at 50 Hertz, you will need a voltage converter.

Outlets in Chile generally accept one type of plug with two round pins (you may see these adapters sold for plug types C & L). If your appliance plug has a different shape, you will need a plug adapter.

Dogs

Stray dogs are everywhere in Chile. You'll see them on the street, around houses, in fields, in short: everywhere. Dogs roam alone and in packs and you'll be surprised just how often you stumble across them. Most are harmless unless provoked but nevertheless merit a wide berth as they will be carrying fleas.

Siesta

Many countries with Spanish origins have an afternoon siesta time. Chile is no exception. However, the traditional siesta (which is usually a nap time after lunch) has changed in practice with a more modern Chile. Depending on where you are in the country, you will see varying manifestations of the siesta. In large urban areas, life may not stop at all after lunch. The smaller a business or store, the more likely they will close for an hour or so after lunch. Even though they may be closed, not many people actually go to sleep. The farther away from Santiago you are, the more likely someone will take a siesta.

Shopping

Chile has various venues to help you buy the things you need: traditional street markets or *ferias;* large supermarkets; and corner stores.

What is *la feria*?

The *feria* is a street market that consists of dozens of individual booths selling all manner of merchandise. An entire street is blocked off for the *feria* and traffic is diverted around this daily market. The *feria* is moved to a different location every day of the week. After one week, the location is back where it started seven days prior.

What can you buy at the *feria*?

The majority of things sold at the *feria* are food. It boasts a wide variety of produce including fruit, vegetables, meats, seafood, and milk.

You can also buy clothes, personal hygiene products, furniture, jewelry, toys, books, and more. Pretty much anything you need (and even stuff you don't) can be bought in the *feria*. The *feria* sings with the shouts of merchants and the buzz of customers shopping and conversing with others.

Who shops at the *feria*?

Since the *feria* moves around daily, there is almost always a day of the week when one is close to your neighborhood. Locals can pick up fresh produce and other commodities they need for the week.

What about the supermarket?

Large supermarkets like Lider, Jumbo, Montserrat, and Unimarc are popping up all over Santiago and other cities across Chile. These are in direct competition with local merchants and the *ferias*. Nevertheless, the *feria* does provide convenience and fresh produce almost on your doorstep.

Corner Stores

Corner stores are where many Chileans purchase their daily bread, food, and other supplies. Some small stores are attached to people's homes and can be found in the middle of neighborhoods or along main roads that lead to housing areas. Chileans will purchase from these stores frequently and will even send their kids down the street to buy what is needed for their family.

Kiosks and Street Vendors

Kiosks adorn many busy street corners. These relatively small newsstands are covered with all the newspapers and magazines they sell. Street vendors can be a good place to find some tasty foods like *empanadas* or a *completo*.

Malls

Chile has a growing number of modern shopping malls like those seen in other countries. These malls, called *mall* or *shopping* by locals, will have large anchor stores and numerous shops in between. Malls will also have food courts where you will find both American fast food chains and some Chilean fast food like *Lomiton* or *Fritz*. Look for Chileanized menus from international brands like Burger King and McDonald's with sandwiches carrying extra mayonnaise and avocado.

Haggling and Negotiation

Depending on where you are spending money, the purchase price may be up for negotiation. The *feria* is a great place to haggle on price for non-food items. In the newer, modern shopping malls and stores, inventory is non-negotiable. Larger ticket items like homes, cars, rent, and similar expenses are open for negotiation.

Writing Dates

Like many parts of the world, Chileans write their dates in the date/month/year format. For example, May 15, 2011 would be written 15/5/2011. This can be confusing if you aren't used to this format.

24-Hour Time

Chileans refer to time by both the 24-hour clock and the 12-hour clock interchangeably. So 7:00 p.m. will be referred to as both 19:00 *horas* and 7:00 *de la tarde*. Official times, particularly those written in print or on screen, like those seen announcing events or TV shows, are usually in 24 hour time. You're more likely to say or hear 12-hour time in conversations with Chileans, though.

Bureaucracy and Receipts

Any official transaction in Chile will involve multiple steps. This is manifested with both simple purchases at the store and when doing complex paperwork with the government.

Typical transactions with the government will require you to go to multiple places to obtain a certain form or signature that you will then take to another location to process. Each step of the way will involve waiting in lines. So if you need to do official business with the government, for example, plan on making a day of it.

This level of formality in official transactions permeates life throughout the country. When you go to a store to purchase something, you will always get a receipt or *boleta* because it is required by law. You will get receipts for everything you purchase, even something small like a piece of candy.

Another side effect of the burden of bureaucracy is the abundance of public notaries. You'll see notaries almost everywhere you look and they may come in handy during your time in Chile. Once something is notarized, it is as good as the original in the eyes of Chileans.

Holidays and Celebrations

Chile has several official annual public holidays. Due to Chile's strong Catholic heritage, many of these holidays have ties to celebrations of the Catholic church.

If a holiday falls on a day of the week near the weekend, Chileans will often take time off and make a "sandwich" day so they can have an extended weekend. The government has also stepped in on occasion to make these sandwich days that bridge the gap between a public holiday and a weekend official holidays, but that isn't always the case.

January 1: New Year's Day - Chile welcomes in the new year with the rest of the world.

March or April: Easter and Holy Week - Traditional Christian holidays celebrating the resurrection of Jesus Christ. Includes Good Friday and the Saturday following.

May 1: Labor Day or Day of the Worker - Celebrates economic and social contributions of workers.

May 21: Navy Day - Commemorates the great naval battle of Iquique and other naval victories.

June 29: Saint Peter and Saint Paul - Catholic feast

celebrating these saints.

July 16: Fiesta de la Virgin del Carmen - Feast celebrated by Catholics.

August 15: Assumption of Mary - Catholic holiday remembering Mary's passage to heaven.

September 18: Independence Day - Chile officially proclaimed independence from Spain on February 12, 1818. Nevertheless, Chileans celebrate their independence on September 18th with the *Fiestas Patrias* since that date was when Chile officially formed its first governing body and began its road to independence.

September 19: Armed Forces Day - Honors the military and their past victories.

October 12: Columbus Day (Day of the Race) - Remembers the day Columbus arrived in the Americas.

October 31: Reformation Day - Day of the Evangelical and Protestant Churches.

November 1: All Saints Day - Catholic holiday celebrating all saints and martyrs.

December 8: Immaculate Conception - Catholic holiday remembering the virgin Mary.

December 25: Christmas Day - Christmas in Chile brings Santa, family time, and fun.

September 11 was once an official holiday commemorating the 1973 military coup that overthrew the socialist President Allende. This date is marred each year by protests, violence, and disturbances. Some animosity towards Americans may be demonstrated on September 11 because the coup was backed by the United States. However, as time goes on, the protests seem to be more opportunistic rioting by those looking for an excuse as opposed to idealistic rebellion. If you are in Chile on this date, be cautious and avoid any riots or large group protests.

Fiestas Patrias

The *fiestas patrias* (literally, "patriotic parties") are a time for all Chileans to gather together and celebrate their country, culture, and independence. These celebrations of *chilenidad*, or Chilean-ness, center around their independence day.

Parade of *Huasos* during *Fiestas Patrias*

Independence Day

Chileans celebrate their independence on the 18th of September. Their road to independence from Spain started on that date in 1810. Although they would have to fight for eight more years to earn their total freedom, Chile celebrates the 18th of 1810 with great fanfare. Chile officially proclaimed independence on February 12, 1818.

The 18th, or *dieciocho*, is celebrated during a week full of *fiestas patrias*. This includes parades, dances, drinking, eating traditional Chilean food, and music.

Parades include *huasos*, the traditional Chilean cowboys, music, and displays of national pride.

Much of the celebrations occur in *ramadas*, temporary open buildings with thatched roofs traditionally made from tree branches. *Ramadas* feature a dance floor, music, and tables to eat at. *Fondas*, or refreshment stands, offer a wide variety of Chilean foods including *empanadas*, *anticuchos* (shish kabobs), *chicha* (alchoholic drink), and more.

There are also frequent dance competitions with the national dance, *la cueca*, being the most popular. Rodeos in their *medialuna* (half-moon) arenas are common in September and showcase the traditional Chilean *huaso*.

September 19

The day after Independence Day is also a national holiday. Armed Forces Day includes military and naval parades and events celebrating Chile's military victories, including their independence.

Chileans enjoy food and music in a *ramada*

Christmas in Chile

Christmas is celebrated in many ways across the varied landscapes and diverse families in Chile. Christmas is often called *Pascua,* which is also the name used for Easter.

Summertime

Since Chile sits in the southern hemisphere, Christmas arrives in the middle of summer. The kids have finished their year of school and enjoy the warmer temperatures and the long summer days.

Santa Claus

Chileans call Santa *Viejito Pascuero* (meaning Old Man Christmas) or even *Papa Noel*. Just like many other countries around the world, he travels by sleigh and reindeer and brings toys and gifts to good boys and girls. Traditionally, he will come in the chimney or climb through the window to deliver his presents. Kids will leave their shoes out so Santa can fill them with goodies, just as stockings are used in other cultures.

Family Time

Christmas is a time when families come together to enjoy each other's company and delicious home-prepared dishes. Many Chilean households consist of several generations and these numbers are augmented at Christmas as other relatives come to visit. People send Christmas cards and buy gifts for friends and loved ones.

Christmas Tree and Decorations

Chileans and Chilean businesses get ready for the big day by decorating. Families put up Christmas trees and decorations. Besides the traditional Christmas tree, you'll see nativity scenes with baby Jesus, Mary, Joseph, the shepherds, animals, and the three wise men.

Christmas Food

Families usually gather together by late afternoon on Christmas Eve to begin the celebrations. A large dinner is served in the late evening. This consists of typical Chilean foods, oven roasted chicken, turkey, or another special meat. *Pan de Pascua*, a sweet fruit cake dessert, is always a staple for this holiday.

A traditional drink called *Cola de Mono* or Monkey's Tail, made from coffee, milk, liquor, cinnamon, and sugar, is served during Christmas time and New Year's.

Christmas Eve

At midnight, gifts are exchanged and opened. Kids may take their new bikes or other toys and head out into the streets to show them off and to play with friends. This excitement is carried over to adults who often stay up late on Christmas Eve celebrating with friends and family.

Christmas Day

Gifts are enjoyed and the children will take their new toys out and play. You will see lots of kids on new bikes and skates. People will also go and visit friends and family during the day. Some families have the tradition of going to the pool or beach on Christmas. For those at home, television channels' programming is filled up with Christmas movies and cartoons.

Most Chileans don't forget that Christmas is centered around Jesus Christ. Many will attend church services including the traditional Christmas Eve mass. Carols are sung and families often read the Bible passages recounting the birth of Jesus.

New Year Celebrations

The New Year begins in Chile at the stroke of midnight on January 1st, just as it does elsewhere around the world.

Chileans like to celebrate the New Year with lots of activities and traditions. Like Christmas, the New Year is a time when family and friends gather together to celebrate.

Since the New Year falls in the middle of Chile's summer, New Year's celebrations spread outside.

The evening of December 31st, the air will be filled with the smells of traditional *asados* (barbecue) with generous servings of meat.

As the clock strikes midnight, friends and family embrace with hugs and give kisses all around. Champagne is shared and toasts are given.

Larger cities in Chile will have massive fireworks shows. Individuals will also buy their own fireworks and use them in their neighborhoods. Watch out if you happen to be on the street on New Year's Eve so you can avoid the bottle rockets that go whizzing by.

New Year's Day is an official national holiday and is usually spent sleeping in to recover from the previous night's festivities.

Birthdays in Chile

Typical birthday gifts include stuffed animals, chocolates, flowers, books, clothing, fragrances, children's toys, other accessories, etc..

Chileans will always sing "*Cumpleaños Feliz*" (Happy Birthday) and if the people in attendance are feeling festive, they will take the birthday person in the middle of the group and throw them up in the air, often as many times as they are years old.

The most typical birthday cakes are pineapple and black forest cakes. The pineapple cake is made of moist cake, filled with whipped cream and pineapple and then decorated with pineapple. The black forest is made of moist chocolate cake and stuffed with raspberry jam and cream, then decorated with chocolate chips and cherries. *Merengue lúcuma* is another popular cake flavor made from the *lúcuma* fruit grown in Chile.

When the birthday person is blowing out the cake, it is tradition to push the cake towards the person so he gets a face full of candles or icing.

Chapter 4: Food

Breakfast

The first meal of the day is small and usually consists of bread with assorted toppings and coffee or tea. Bread is bought fresh daily from a corner bakery, a local shop, or even a bread salesman that travels around the neighborhood. Chileans will top their bread with jelly or a delicious caramel-like topping called *manjar*.

Lunch

The largest meal of the day is usually lunch. This will consist of traditional Chilean dishes like *cazuela* (a stew), *pastel de choclo* (similar to shepherd or meat pie), or a wide variety of bean dishes. In rural areas, the lunch hour usually means businesses will close.

Once (pronounced own-say)

Once is a light meal that is eaten between 4 and 7 in the afternoon. Often this is a repeat of breakfast, with bread and sandwich toppings with some tea or coffee.

Tradition has it that long ago men who wanted to drink their liquor, or *aguardiente*, during the time of day that is now *once* invented a code to hide the fact that they were drinking at 5:00 in the afternoon. This code was the number of letters in *aguardiente,* which is eleven—or *once* in Spanish. With the passage of time, tea time became known as *once.*

Dinner

Dinner comes in the late evening and will be the size of lunch with traditional Chilean food. If most in the household work all day, dinner for them will be the largest meal. Don't be surprised to be eating dinner after 9:00 or even 10:00 in the evening. Depending on how busy the family is, *once* and dinner may be combined into one meal.

Cazuela de Vacuno

Typical Chilean Dishes

Anticuchos - shish kabobs made of skewered meat, onions, and other vegetables

Barros Jarpa – sandwich with ham and melted cheese

Barros Luco – sandwich with steak and melted cheese

Bistec a lo Pobre - Steak topped with french fries and/or fried onions and fried eggs

Cazuela - Traditional Chilean soup made from cooking several meats and vegetables together

Completos - Hot dogs on an oversized bun, served with mustard, mayo, tomatoes, sauerkraut and avocado

Curanto – typical slow cooked seafood dish of shellfish, potatoes, and vegetables

Empanadas de Pino - Turnovers stuffed with diced beef, onions, raisins, olives, and hard-boiled egg and baked in an oven

Delicious oven-baked empanadas

Empanadas de Queso - Turnovers filled with cheese and usually fried

Parrillada / Asasdos - Traditional cook-out with a variety of meats and sausages grilled outside over coals

Pastel de Choclo

Pastel de Choclo - Made from fresh ground corn (choclo) with basil

Pebre - Condiment made of coriander, chopped onion, chopped tomato, cilantro, olive oil, garlic and ground or pureed spicy aji peppers. This can be spicy—so be ready.

Porotos Granados - Hot bean dish made with corn and pumpkin

Chilean Barbecue (*Asado*)

One of the great Chilean traditions during the *fiestas patrias* and summer months is the Chilean barbecue, called an *asado*.

The *asado* is more that just cooking outside. It is a social event that is a key part of the Chilean culture. Friends and family will gather frequently for *asados* and it is a great place to socialize.

Part of the social experience is having the grill master, typically a male, tend to the grill while drinking and talking with others. The women of the house are often found inside making salads and other side dishes.

You won't find gas grills at a typical *asado*. The preferred method of grilling is over a wood fire and then the resulting coals. The grills range from a simple stand-alone metal grill, to fire pits with large grates placed over them.

At a typical Chilean barbeque, you will enjoy skewers (the typical *anticucho*, or shish kabobs, include beef pieces intermixed with sausage, vegetables, or other meats cooked on a skewer), sausage (*chorizo* or spicy pork sausage), *choripan* (*chorizo* inside *marraqueta* bread), chicken, and steaks.

These main meat dishes are often accompanied by Chilean salad (a tomato and onion dish) and bread.

Alcoholic Drinks

Chile is a producer of world class wines that rank with those from France, Italy, and California. You'll find wines in traditional glass bottles but also cheaper variants in carton boxes.

Beer is consumed in social settings, at *fútbol* games, and in the home. Cristal is a popular Chilean beer that also sponsors many events and sports teams.

Chicha is made from fermented grapes and is a traditional drink most commonly consumed during Chile's *fiestas patrias*, celebrating their independence.

Pisco Sour is considered the national drink of Chile. This cocktail contains *pisco* (liquor from grapes), lemon or lime juice, egg whites, simple syrup, and regional bitters.

Coffee and Tea

Coffee and tea are constant staples of life in Chile. They are served most frequently at breakfast and *once*. In homes, coffee is typically made from instant coffee granules like those offered by Nescafé or wheat-based coffee like Ecco. Tea is usually made in individual servings and you'll often have a variety of herbal teas available.

Milk

Milk is sold in box cartons on the shelf at the grocery or corner store. This milk doesn't need to be refrigerated until it is opened. Milk isn't typically served as a drink by itself except to children or when heated up as hot chocolate.

Water

Tap water in Chile is safe to drink. It may take a few days for your body to get accustomed to it, but overall, it is safe. That being said, Chileans will almost never serve you a glass of water. Instead they will serve you juice (usually made from a powder concentrate) or a carbonated drink. If you ask for water at a restaurant, you'll get bottled water, typically *agua mineral* with carbonation. If you like your water without the bubbles, be sure to ask for *agua sin gas* (or without gas).

Bebidas

Chileans love Coca Cola. It is everywhere and is consumed from an early age (even in baby bottles). You'll be served Coke a lot, and if you don't want that, you'll be offered Fanta (the orange carbonated drink) as an alternative. These drinks are often sold in one or two liter bottles that have to be returned for a deposit or simply traded in for the next purchase. Be sure to try Chile's own Bilz or Pap drinks for a local spin on the *bebida.*

Diet Drinks in Chile

Don't expect to use the literal translation of diet—or *dieta*—attached to the drink name.

Diet drinks in Chile have the the English word "Light" on them.

So if you want a Diet Coke, ask for a "Coca-Cola Light." Of course, you'll also find several brands that use the "Zero" label for zero calorie drinks, like Coca-Cola Zero.

Typical Chilean Desserts

A tantalizing Berlin

Berlin - Round doughnut filled with *manjar*, jelly, or custard and topped with powdered sugar

Kuchen – cake originated from German ancestry usually contains fruit

Mote con Huesillo - Dehydrated peaches with stewed barley often in water or peach juice

Alfajor – Round, flat, cookie-like pastry filled with *manjar* and covered in chocolate

Fruit

Chile produces a wide range of fresh fruit that you may have already tried from your local grocer, since fruit is one of Chile's main international exports. The familiar fruits, like fresh grapes, kiwis, figs, apples, berries, pears, and apricots are plentiful. In addition, you'll discover some new fruits like chirimoya (custard apple), papaya, lúcuma, membrillo, and tuna (prickly pear). Fruit is extremely cheap in Chile, especially when compared to the imported prices you probably pay at home.

Bread

Chileans eat bread all day long. It is the primary substance of breakfast and *once*, and will accompany lunch and dinner as well. Bread is baked fresh twice daily at local bakeries and is purchased daily for consumption. In fact, Chileans eat over 200 pounds (90 kilograms) of bread a year which puts them as some of the highest consumers of bread in the world.

Marraqueta bread

You'll find several types of bread in Chile: *marraquetas* (a crunchy french-like bread), *hallulla* (flat round bread), *pan amasado* (a thick, homemade tasting bread), and even *pan de molde* (boxed shape bread loaves).

69

Seafood

Chile has one of the longest coastlines in the world, which naturally yields plenty of seafood. The farther south you visit in the country, the more common seafood will be as a main dish. Expect all types of seafood, including salmon, trout, flounder, eel, oysters, crabs, scallops, clams, seaweed, mussels, octopus, and sea urchins.

Congor Eel

Eating Out

Chileans tend to linger at restaurants to socialize. You'll need to ask the server for your bill as it won't necessarily be brought out to you immediately. Tip your server 10% of the bill.

Chapter 5: Money

Chilean Peso

From México down to Colombia and then on to Argentina, the peso is the standard monetary unit. Although several Latin American countries use currency called the peso, they are not all the same. The Chilean peso is, of course, what is used in Chile. There are several paper bills as well as a pocketful of coins.

The Chilean peso is fairly stable with a good exchange rate with the US dollar and Euro.

Chile finally gained independence from Spain in 1818 after the battle of Maipú. At this time, the first coin of an independent Chile became the silver peso minted in 1817 (see
image to the right). With the establishment of the decimal system in 1851, Chile started minting its first copper coins.

In 1975, the peso replaced the escudo (that in 1960 had replaced the old peso), with one peso equal to 1000 escudos.

The Chilean Peso uses the dollar sign $.

Decimals, Not Commas

When you see prices listed in Chile, don't be confused to see a decimal where you expected to see a comma. One thousand is written 1.000, not 1,000. In typical day-to-day purchases, you'll never see fractions of a peso as you may see fractions of a dollar as cents in the United States.

Paper Money

Bills come in denominations of $1.000, $2.000, $5.000, $10.000, and $20.000 Pesos. In 2009, the Central Bank of Chile started releasing new versions of the Peso banknotes with enhanced anti-forgery features. You'll see a mix of old and new banknotes during the next several years as the old bills are slowly retired.

$1.000 Pesos

$2.000 Pesos

$5.000 Pesos

$10.000 Pesos

$20.000 Pesos

If you want a crash course in famous Chileans, look no further than their paper currency. The $1.000 peso bill shows Ignacio Carrera Pinto, hero of Chile's War of the Pacific against Bolivia and Peru. The $2.000 bill features Manuel Rodríguez Erdoyza, one of Chile's founding fathers. Nobel prize winning poet, Gabriela Mistral, graces the $5.000 note. Arturo Prat Chacón, naval captain and hero of the War of the Pacific, sits on the

$10.000 bill. Andrés Bello, although Venezuelan by birth, founded the University of Chile and adorns the $20.000 peso note.

Coin Money

Coins come in all shapes, sizes and values. There are peso coins in denominations of 1, 5, 10, 50, 100, and 500 pesos. The 1 and 5 peso coins are almost never used since they are almost worthless.

Chilean Peso Coins (not to scale)

The 1, 5, 10, and 50 pesos coins all have the image of Chile's liberator, Bernardo O'Higgins. The older 100 pesos coin shows the Chilean national seal. Relatively newer coins for the 100 and 500 pesos have images of a native Mapuche woman and Cardinal Raúl Silva Henríquez, respectively.

Access to Money

In Santiago, exchange houses are plentiful in the financial district, in most city centers, shopping malls, and airports. They will be able to exchange dollars and euros for Chilean pesos. Chile also has many ATMs that will let you withdraw needed funds (in Chilean pesos) using your foreign ATM card.

How to Pay

Major stores, hotels, and airlines will take credit cards as payment. With smaller retailers, corner stores, street markets, and others, you'll need cash to pay for goods or services.

IVA Tax

Chile has a tax called *Impuesto al Valor Agregado*–commonly referred to as IVA—that is built into the price of almost everything you buy.

Other countries call this tax the Value Add Tax (VAT) or Goods and Services Tax (GST).

IVA in Chile is a flat 19%. You won't see this amount broken out on receipts because it is included in the price of goods and services you purchase.

As a foreigner, you can be exempt from paying IVA in one situation: your hotel lodging.

If you pay for your hotel with foreign currency (like US dollars or euros) or with a foreign-issued credit card, you will not have to pay IVA.

There are some caveats to this exemption. Your hotel will have to be registered with Chile's SII (Internal Tax Service) and you will most likely have to get your passport photocopied. So if you stay at smaller lodging that perhaps hasn't registered with the SII, you may not get the exemption.

Even as a foreigner, you'll pay IVA on all other purchases.

When you pay for your hotel or lodging, make sure to ask if IVA is included in the rate you pay. Ask for the discount if you are paying with foreign currency or credit card. You shouldn't have to do any paperwork other than prove you are a foreigner. That's why you'll need to present your passport and the tourist visa that you get upon arrival in the country.

Chapter 6: Travel

Santiago Transit

Santiago has an extensive public transportation system so many people take the bus or subway to work or across town.

In 2005, Santiago began a major upgrade of its public transportation system known as Transantiago. This system aimed to correct the problems of the older system via new buses, routes, payment options, and technology. Unfortunately, things haven't gone very well with Transantiago and it has created lots of problems for Santiago residents who need to catch a bus. You may want to avoid that hassle and take a cab, the metro, or rent a car.

Metro

Santiago has a very modern, clean, and efficient underground subway system known as the Metro.

Metro Station

The Metro is an integral part of Santiago's overall public transportation system. The Metro lines are centered in downtown Santiago and spread outward towards the suburbs.

The Metro's system of lines and stations is slowly spreading across most of Santiago. The Metro currently has five lines in operation and is expanding its system to reach even farther outward from the city center.

The Metro system utilizes a varying fare rate based on the time of day you travel. Prices are higher during peak rush hours (7:00-9:00 and 18:00-20:00) and lower in the middle of the day, evenings, and weekends. Fares average around $500 pesos or about US$1. Discounts are given to students and senior citizens.

Micros

Micro in Santiago

The *micro* (pronounced 'ME-crow') is the main source of public transportation in the city. It is cheap, and you'll see them all over the city. They are not owned by the city or government, but are privately owned by different companies.

Micros stop at *paraderos* (bus stops) that are roughly every 5-10 blocks. The *paradero* numbers decrease the closer you get to the center of town. On smaller roads, the driver will stop wherever you want. Just press the *timbre* (a buzzer) to let the driver know you want to get off.

Long Range Buses

A popular way to travel between cities and to the far reaches of the country is by bus. These long range buses offer better seating than their micro counterparts and run on regular schedules. Turbus and Pullman are well-known long range bus companies in Chile.

Taxis

Most taxis are black with yellow roofs. Just like anywhere else, they are the most expensive mode of public transportation. However, taxis are relatively cheap in Chile when compared to other countries. A 20-25 minute ride will be less than US$20.

While it may be customary to tip the taxi driver in most places around the world, this is not the case in Chile.

In Chile, most taxis are driven by the vehicle owners and so the fares they earn are theirs to keep.

Feel free to round up the fare to an easier peso amount to pay but don't feel obligated to pay a gratuity on top of that.

If you plan on taking a taxi in Chile, be sure you have plenty of smaller peso bills and some peso coins to make paying easier. *Taxistas* won't always have change for larger bills.

Collectivos

Collectivos look like taxis but they run along set routes like a bus. These are typically sedans although you may see the occasional van. *Collectivos* display their major route milestones on a sign on the roof of the vehicle. They are more expensive than the *micros* because once they fill up, they don't stop for new passengers.

Train

Although Chile used to have a very extensive railway system, this is no longer as reliable and cheap as the long range buses. You can find trains from Santiago that head south with the most reliable and quick route between Santiago and Chillán. Additionally, you'll find the Metrotren quite reliable as it runs between Santiago and some communities south of the city.

Boat

Cruise lines frequently stop in Chile's port cities of Valparaíso and the southern Punta Arenas. You will also find cruises of Chile's Patagonia and glaciers that leave from Puerto Montt and other southern port cities.

Driving in Chile

If you, as a visitor, want to drive in Chile, you technically need an international driver's license. However, in practice, your existing license may suffice. Your biggest challenge on the road will be the *micro* drivers, who drive a little crazy.

Be sure to keep within the speed limits and posted traffic signs. Chile's police force, *los Carabineros*, are usually out in force. If you get a ticket, they will literally take away your license and you'll have to go to court to get it back and pay for your ticket.

Don't try to bribe the police! *Carabineros* are an honest, trustworthy police force who don't fit the stereotypical, crooked South American police officer image.

Parking Attendants

If you are driving in Chile, you'll need to park your car. Don't be surprised to find parking attendants awaiting your arrival. They may not look official but you should tip them anyway.

International Air Travel

Many international airlines offer flights to and from Chile. Most flights originate or end at Santiago's International Airport. You'll also find several smaller carriers that serve South American countries.

Domestic Air Travel

Chile has two major domestic airlines: Lan and Sky. These are your best bet for air travel within the country as they offer multiple daily flights to the far reaches of Chile. Their best fares are only available for purchase within Chile and in Chilean pesos.

Santiago Airport

The Santiago International Airport, named "Com. Arturo Merino Benitez" after a pioneer in Chilean air transportation, sits on the northwest side of Santiago. Most international flights arrive into Chile via this airport. Santiago's airport code is SCL. Santiago's airport has a very modern, clean, and efficient terminal.

Taxes and Fees

All passengers with passports from Australia, Canada, the United States and Mexico must pay a reciprocity tax upon arrival in Chile (Australia US$61, Canada US$132, United States US$131, Mexico US$23). These taxes fluctuate based on the exchange rate so it may be a little more or less than these prices.

This reciprocity fee is called such because Chilean citizens are required to pay to visit these same countries. Once you've paid the reciprocity fee and have had it documented, the receipt issued is valid for the life of your passport and you won't need to pay the fee again if you enter Chile again.

Domestic flights carry an airport tax of about US$18 that is usually included in the ticket price.

Ground Transportation

There are numerous ways to get from the Santiago airport to your final destination. These include taxis, buses, shuttles, and rental cars.

Major Airports

Although Chile's major international airport is in Santiago, there are several other main airports. These airports have services such as international police, immigration, customs, restaurants, bathrooms, gift shops, and news stands. Mostly domestic flights travel to these airports.

Chile's other major airports are:
- Arica (Chacalluta)
- Antofagasta (Cerro Moreno)
- Iquique (Cavancha)
- Puerto Montt (Tepual)
- Punta Arenas (Pdte. Ibañez)
- Temuco (Manquehue)

Chapter 7: Communicating

Understanding

Your biggest problem with Spanish in Chile will not be speaking but rather understanding what is being said. Chilean Spanish is said to be difficult even for native Spanish speakers to understand. If you have taken Spanish classes in the past, that is a great start. But it will take you a while to orient yourself to the nuances of Spanish in Chile, known locally as *Castellano*.

Words ending in -ado become -ao

There is a tendency for words that end in -ado to be reduced to -ao where the "d" sound drops out. Chileans like to talk fast! For example:

- pasado = pasao
- Example: el tiempo ya está pasao
- lado = lao
- Example: se encuentra al otro lao

Drop the final "s"

Chileans tend to omit the final letter "s" on words. For example:

- más o menos = má o meno

Familiar verb conjugation: "vos"

The familiar form of addressing a person in Spanish is "tú." This is usually conjugated like this:

- hablar (to speak) = tú hablas (you speak)
- vivir (to live) = tú vives (you live)
- querer (to want) = tú quieres (you want)

However, Chileans like to use a customized version of the tú form. This is "vos," which you may hear as "vo." This form is created by conjugating the verb in vosotros and then dropping the final 's'. The aforementioned examples become the following when using "vos":

- hablar (to speak) = hablái (you speak)
- vivir (to live) = viví (you live)
- querer (to want) = queréi (you want)

Ending phrases with "po"

"Po" is a derivative of the Spanish "pues" that is often used as a link between sentences or phrases in speaking. "Po" gets thrown on the end of many things, though, without connecting sentences or phrases. For example:

- ¿Cómo estás? Bien po.
- ¿Fuiste al mercado? Sí, po.

Everything is Small

Chileans love to use the diminutive with words to show endearment or just because. Everywhere you turn something ends in -cito or -ito. This literally translated makes the noun "very small" even though it isn't literally that. For example, if you want a coffee, it may very well be a *cafecito*. Because of its frequent use, this may also make words that don't literally make sense when you translate them. For example, a fat person may be called *gordito* which literally means little fat.

Tú vs. Usted

The Spanish language can translate the singular "you" into the informal *tú* or the formal *usted.* So which one should you use in Chile? With kids, close friends, and family, use *tú*. With household servants, people older than you, in the workplace, and when meeting people for the first time in a formal setting, use *usted.*

You may find yourself being called *tú* by someone, for example, an elderly woman, that you should respond to with *usted*. Follow the lead of the Chileans around you and you should be fine most of the time.

Third Person

Chileans like to refer to people in the 3rd person by adding an article to their name. For example, if we're talking about José, he may be referred to as *el José*.

Leísmo

Chileans will replace the direct object pronouns *lo* and *la* with the indirect object pronoun *le*. For example, "I see the boy" is *Yo veo al niño,* which becomes *Yo le veo.*

Slang

Chilean vocabulary is rich in slang terms and phrases that only those in Chile understand. If you are to successfully understand what people are saying to you or even read newspaper headlines, you'll need to pick up some slang. The more phrases you know, the more impressed your Chilean friends will be. Mastering Chilean slang is a true sign that you literally know what you're talking about.

Here are 31 slang phrases that you'll find helpful:
1. Al tiro - immediately
2. ¡Bakan! - very cool
3. ¡Buena onda! - cool, great
4. no cacha ni uno - He doesn't understand a thing
5. ¿cachai? - do you understand?
6. capo - good at something, smart
7. cara de palo - boldly, frankly
8. cuestión - thing, matter
9. dejar la escoba - to leave a mess, disaster
10. encachado - good looking
11. ¡no estoy ni ahí! - I don't care
12. fome - boring, stupid
13. gamba - your foot, or the 100 peso coin
14. guagua - a baby
15. harto - a lot
16. lolo(a) - a teenager
17. luca - 1000 peso bill
18. medio(a) - very big
19. pata de vaca (said "pate vaca") - to act badly or to have bad intentions
20. pega - work, job
21. pegar en la pera - to mooch, to eat and socialize, take advantage of
22. pesado - mean, rude, bothersome

23. pescar + "algo" - to pay attention to, to notice
24. pololo(a) - boyfriend / girlfriend
25. ¡Que choro! - entertaining, worthy of attention
26. no salvar a nadie - to be worthless, useless
27. sapear - to be nosy, eavesdrop
28. se cree la muerte - you think you are better than everyone else
29. tener el diente largo - To be very hungry, so hungry I could eat a horse
30. hacer tuto - take a nap
31. weón - depending on use: either an idiot or something you'd call a friend, like "buddy"

Conclusion

You now know more about Chile and the Chilean culture than 95% of people who visit this amazing country. In fact, you may even know a thing or two that some Chileans don't even know.

By internalizing the topics discussed here, you will be prepared to get the most out of your time in Chile, be that one day or several years.

During your time in Chile, soak in the culture that you experience. Make note of the quirks, nuances, and oddities that you discover. These unique, individual characteristics are what make Chile so special.

Enjoy your time in Chile, and you too will repeat the shout you will hear chanted on the streets or during *fútbol* games:

CHI-CHI-CHI-LE-LE-LE

¡VIVA CHILE!

Additional Reading

Visit the Pepe's Chile website for a vast collection of information about Chilean culture and travel:

http://pepeschile.com

If you are interested in learning more about Chile, these books will also help you:

Travel Guides

- *Fodor's Chile*
  http://amzn.to/eAkcWs
- *Chile & Easter Island (Country Guide)*
  http://amzn.to/fwTh46
- *Frommer's Chile & Easter Island*
  http://amzn.to/gopN1D

Chilean Spanish

- *Chilenismos: A Dictionary and Phrasebook for Chilean Spanish*
  http://amzn.to/hm83ho
- *How to Survive in the Chilean Jungle*
  http://amzn.to/evErBK

Food

- *Tasting Chile: A Celebration of Authentic Chilean Foods and Wines*
  http://amzn.to/fOzFCR
- *Three Generations of Chilean Cuisine*
  http://amzn.to/gLn4Gz

- *Knack South American Cooking*
  http://amzn.to/fsKc2v

History

- *The History of Chile (Palgrave Essential Histories)*
  http://amzn.to/gRGi6h

Glossary

abrazo - hug

aguardiente - liquor

Araucanos – original, native people of Chile

asado – cook-out, barbeque

baby fútbol - mini-soccer

blocks - apartments

cafecito - coffee

califont – water heater

canchas – courts/fields (like for soccer)

Carabineros – national police force

Castellano – Spanish as it is known in Chile

chilenidad – Chilean national identity

Cola de Mono - "Tail of a monkey", traditional Christmas drink

Collectivos – taxi-like public transportation

cueca – national dance of Chile

dieciocho - 18th

estufa – stove / space heater

feria – open air street market

fiestas patrias – independence day celebrations

fondas – gathering place for celebrating fiestas patrias

fútbol - soccer

gordito - fatty

gringo – non-Latin person, usually a westerner, like American or European

gringolandia – reference to the United States

halo – yelled to get someone to come to the door

huasos – traditional Chilean cowboys

machismo – assertive masculinity, male chauvinism

medialuna – half-moon stadium for rodeos

micro - bus

nanas - maid

once – tea time meal

Papa Noel – Santa Claus

paraderos – bus stops

parcelas – typical plots of land around country estates

Pascua – Easter / Christmas

ramadas – gathering place for celebrating fiestas patrias

Santiaguinos – residents of Santiago

temblores - tremor

terremotos - earthquake

timbre – buzzer (on a bus)

tío or tía – uncle or aunt

Viejito Pascuero – Santa Claus

Photo Credits

Viña del Mar: http://www.flickr.com/photos/soschilds/376251138/

Santiago: http://www.flickr.com/photos/patrickcoe/862384305/

Easter Island: http://www.flickr.com/photos/philliecasablanca/2052720494/

Atacama: http://www.flickr.com/photos/alita/2516666242/

Volcan Osorno: http://www.flickr.com/photos/sarahandiain/363643687/

Torres del Paine: http://flickr.com/photos/gcourbis/376610888/

Copihue: http://www.flickr.com/photos/inaovas/5087642130/

Chuquicamata: http://flickr.com/photos/jimmybyrum/3382840065/

The Atacama Desert: http://flickr.com/photos/ogwen/2807235438/

Volcán Osorno: http://flickr.com/photos/bitterroot/103936558/

Andes Mountains: http://flickr.com/photos/aldeasim/233344281/

Chilean Coast near Viña del Mar: http://flickr.com/photos/loco085/2108877416/

Dancing la cueca in traditional huaso attire:
http://flickr.com/photos/mabel_de_todo_un_poco/1333691388/

Un abrazo: http://flickr.com/photos/nestorcarrasco/2375496605/

A Game of Soccer: http://flickr.com/photos/empezardecero/3301019619/

Row houses in Valparaiso: http://flickr.com/photos/blmurch/399240869/

Cazuela de Vacuno: http://flickr.com/photos/peterme/298715185

Delicious empanadas:
http://flickr.com/photos/mabel_de_todo_un_poco/1384634772/

Pastel de Choclo: http://flickr.com/photos/palomabaytelman/2061134471/

A tantalizing Berlin: http://flickr.com/photos/peregrineblue/2343545389/

Metro Station: http://flickr.com/photos/empezardecero/2298355911/

About the Author

Joe Rawlinson lived in Chile for two years and fell in love with the Chilean people and this beautiful country. Since 1998, he has helped thousands of people like you learn more about this wonderful country via his Pepe's Chile website: http://pepeschile.com.

Printed in Great Britain
by Amazon.co.uk, Ltd.,
Marston Gate.